Fund Your Dreams!

Proven Tools for Pitching Investors

K.C. Hildreth

Published by Hildreth Consulting, Los Angeles, CA

www.kchildreth.com

ISBN:
ISBN-13: 978-1497378605
ISBN 10: 1497378605

DEDICATION

To Neha. Your love and support makes everything possible.

ACKNOWLEDGEMENTS

Special thanks to my clients, friends and family. I am very grateful for your unswerving encouragement and support.

OTHER BOOKS BY K.C. HILDRETH

Supercharge Your Startup!
Creating a Powerful Vision and Business Plan in 5 Easy Steps

Living Into Your Highest Potential
3 Key Steps to Personal Growth

CONTENTS

PREFACE

This book is one of a series of books on Success, Entrepreneurship, Organizational Culture, and, in the future, many other topics related to human creativity, performance and growth. All of my books are intended as an introduction to topics that can be, and I believe should be, explored in more detail. For ease of access they are purposefully short and easy to digest. I encourage you to test, explore and learn more about each topic so that you can expand upon what I have written. In my work with clients I stress that the process of learning and growing is highly unique to each person and occurs best when *you decide you want to expand*. If you want the knowledge in this book to trigger something, then it will. I can only offer you the processes and information that I know to be effective. I hope it works for you!

If you need help, I am available.

K.C. Hildreth

www.kchildreth.com

INTRODUCTION

If you are reading this book, then you likely have an idea that you would like to pitch to an investor. Congratulations! This is a great place to be! Even better, there are millions of dollars waiting to help you in your quest. You merely have to develop the ability to attract that money into your venture. I have done this many times, raising tens of millions of dollars for companies that I founded or helped to get off the ground. This e-book will show you how you can do it for yourself.

The most exciting time for any entrepreneur is the beginning, because this is when all the future potential of your idea is contained in your mind. Everything is possible. Your idea, the picture of what 'can be', exists as a thought form inside of you that is in the process of becoming manifest, or 'real' in the world. To see something before it is real is exciting and wondrous because it is an invitation to create, an opportunity to exercise the power of manifestation.

Your idea represents the very essence of creation. In fact, everything physical in the universe began first as an idea…a thought that in-formed the shape and order of molecules and structures. Without this information the universe would appear random and unstructured. Instead of spherical planets, elliptical orbits and a definable table of elements, for example, we might see a host of strangely shaped objects comprised of ever changing molecules moving randomly about the universe. Fundamental, information-based forces in the universe, such as gravity, in-formed the way matter organized. Because of this all of the planets and stars and physical celestial objects coalesced in a similar manner: Spherical, rotating and attracted to each other. Your thoughts create structure in the same way.

Even more powerfully, among animals we humans have been endowed with the unique ability to direct our consciousness in order to generate a particular outcome. We can conceptualize something (have an idea), intend toward a specific outcome, and then take action to turn the idea into something real…to *create*. The toothbrush you used this morning? At some point in history a person felt gunk on his/her teeth and looked around for a tool to scrape away the discomfort. Perhaps it was a piece of moss on a stick…or a bit of rough animal hide. In either case he/she pictured the tool he/she needed and created an object that matched the concept in his/her head. And thus the idea of 'toothbrush' was made manifest. A thought was brought into the physical world.

The idea you have in this moment is a thought-form at the first stages of creation. You are holding a picture in your head that, when brought into existence, will change the physical world forever. Even if your thought is not 'successful', it will have added to the collective knowledge of humanity and advanced the universe itself. As a creative being you have an impact. Your thoughts matter because they influence and improve the nature of the world. You don't need to do much more than believe in your idea, believe in yourself, strongly intend to make your thoughts a physical reality, and act!

This brings me back to investors. Making your idea 'real' requires action, and action requires resources. You need food, sleep and energy to take the actions that ultimately result in a 'creation'. You also will likely need help from other human beings who can add their creative power to your efforts in order to improve and speed-up the outcome. This collaboration can come in the form of ideas, supportive work, or money. The purpose of this book is to teach you how to secure the latter...to show you how to share your idea in such a way as to inspire others to offer you the money you need to create. This is the key point I want you to understand: When you seek investment you are *asking others to participate in your vision*, to add their creative energy to your own. They must feel a part of your quest, a partner in your vision. Without this feeling they will sense that you only want their money, and this will drive them away.

Inspiring others to share in your excitement is a skill that can be learned, but it also must be practiced. You will need to learn how to tell a story in such a way as to become compelling, and this requires that you believe deeply in yourself and your idea. When you believe, *really believe*, in your idea and your ability to create you harness an energy that is both powerful and infectious. When you tell your story from this place people will feel excitement and inspiration. They will see our creative power and will want to be a part of what you are doing.

Making your story compelling requires that you take the content (your idea and plan), organize it in a way that makes it easy to digest, and then deliver it with energy and passion. When you do this effectively the impact is profound. Listeners will be swept up in the wave of excitement that you generate and ask you how they can become involved. Your message may not reach 100% of the people with whom you speak, but it will reach many more than if you had just 'winged it' and offered a bland assessment of your project.

I have personally raised millions of dollars using the techniques you will learn in this book. In 2001 I helped raise $35 million dollars at a time when the economy and stock market were both in free-fall. What I learned along the way is that a good idea is worth only so much…the power to raise money comes mostly from the ability to generate excitement and desire in those who can help. This book will teach you how.

THE PLAN

Contrary to what you may think, your business plan is not the reason an investor will give you his or her money. Your plan will get you in the door and help you make a compelling argument about the nature of your business, but the content of your document merely organizes the details behind the story you will be telling. That being said you cannot pitch an idea without a plan, so it is very important to think carefully about what you intend to include.

One of the most powerful results of working on a business plan is the expertise that it creates in *you*. In order to write a plan you must learn about the industry, think about your strategy, come up with pricing models, and research a range of subjects related to your idea. When you do this you become educated about what you intend to do, and *this* is why an investor will give you his or her money. When you become an expert in your field then people trust you, and when they trust you they are willing to invest their money in your ideas.

I have written an entire book on business plans, and so will only summarize the content of a plan in this section. For more detailed information please see "Supercharge Your Startup: Creating a Powerful Vision and Business Plan in 5 Easy Steps".

In short, a plan must answer, at a minimum, certain questions in an order that drives the most interest. An ideal plan would have the following sections:

1. **The idea.** What is the idea? What is the mission and vision of the company (in short)? Why is it compelling?
2. **The market.** How big is the market? Who buys the product? (age, gender, demographics) Why do they buy it?
3. **The product.** What are you offering, and in what variations? Why is it interesting?
4. **Operations.** How do you intend to make the product? What machines are you going to need? Where will you get your raw material? How are you going to keep and manage inventory? How do you intend to service your product (returns, etc)?
5. **Technology** (for web sites). What capabilities will your web site have? Will people be able to buy from it?
6. **Marketing and Sales.** How do you intend on selling your product (ie internet or other)? Will you sell direct or through retail channels? How do you intend on marketing your company and product (ie internet, advertising, other)? If a consumer product, how will it be branded? Are there any special strategies to sell your product?

7. **Business Model** (this is linked to the spreadsheet). How do you intend to price the product (ie low cost provider, or high end, or both)? Where will most of your revenues come from? Where will most of your costs come from? What will be your profit margin? Why are you going to make a boat-load of money?

8. **Strategy and competitive landscape.** Who else is doing this? What are they doing? How much business do they do? Why are you different or special? Why is there room for you too?

9. **Financing needs and Corporate Structure.** How is the company organized (corporate structure)? Where are you going to get your initial capital? How much more money are you going to need? How will you manage cash flows? Are you looking for outside investors?

10. **Bios**. Who is involved? Why are they qualified to do this?

These questions are generally answered in two sections: The body and the supporting spreadsheets. The body is, essentially, the written answers to these questions. The spreadsheets are the numbers that back up your written statements. For example, as you research your industry you are going to find out its size (number of units sold annually and total revenues) and the market demographics (who buys it). Given these global numbers you will assume that you can capture a certain portion of that market, a percentage that you will 'own'. Your spreadsheet provides the numbers around your assumptions and supports your written statements.

As an investor looks over your plan (they will rarely read the whole thing) they will bounce from the written document to the spreadsheets and back again. Most investors are trying to see if a) you did your homework, and b) your argument (the strategy and numbers) make sense. The first step in this process is sometimes called 'the sniff test'. If it looks reasonable then you go on to the next step. If not, you will be turned down. Being thorough in your research is imperative to being considered, so take it seriously.

When you have answered all of the questions and provided reasonable revenue and costs estimates, then you may be asked to tell your story. This is 'the pitch' where you get to verbally convey your idea and plans. In this process many questions will be asked about your assumptions, so you must know every detail and have thought through most of the objections. Investors, especially professionals, are notoriously impatient. If you don't know what you are talking about you will be quickly shown the door.

THE STORY

At this point your plan (or a summary of the plan) has elicited enough interest to get you in the door of a potential investor. Now what? You know you need to get this person(s) excited about your idea, but also want to do so in a way that is both professional and compelling. This moment, called 'the pitch', is the most important and pivotal point in the entire process.

In order to create a compelling pitch you need to first consider how people learn and how they like to consume information. For thousands of years our ancestors sat around fires telling each other stories. Some of these tales involved historical events, others moral lessons, and still others descriptions of the natural world and its workings. Yet no matter the content of the story, human beings have known that to affect an audience, to have them connect and remember the facts, the tale must be compelling and interesting and 'resonant'. When listeners are absorbed by a story they identify with it. In this identification they are attracted to both the speaker and to the ideas the speaker is sharing.

So if you want to sell an idea, tell a good story. Craft your content in a way that hooks the reader, connects them to your line of thinking, and then inspires them to continue the journey in their own minds. Every movie, book and tale tries to do this. Myths, described by Joseph Campbell in 'The Power of Myth", are one of the most powerful storytelling mechanisms. The 'hero's journey' is one of these myths and can be easily identified in most adventure movies. The hero ventures out, faces challenges, questions him/herself, becomes something larger, then comes home. This story 'arc' is one to which every human being can relate. So when you create your story you want to tap into a similar arc. Every person on the planet wants to be excited about something, to hear a story of possibility and hope. Your job is to tell this story.

Your tale of possibility, your 'story arc', should have three main components.

1. **The idea and its origin.** This is the 'Genesis story' and is represented in every human religion. Every creative act has a source, and we humans are endlessly curious about the origins of such things. When did your idea occur to you? How did you feel as it happened? What did you conclude? Why was it powerful to you? When you can help people feel what you felt at the 'birthing moment', you hook them into your story. Even if they don't agree or are uncertain about your concept, they will want to hear more. When a Genesis

story is told well and with excitement people almost always stick around to see if there might just be brilliance behind the words.

2. **Making the idea a reality.** This is the 'how' of your plan. How are you going to make or offer what you are proposing? How are you going to sell it? Who will buy it? What is going to be required to make all this happen? Who are the people involved? This section must be simple yet thorough. When you tell a 'business story' you must at a minimum talk about marketing, operations, technology, manufacturing, competitors and finances...all the things you have already analyzed in your plan. In this section you must be ready for spontaneous questions, so be prepared!

3. **A vision of a powerful outcome.** This is the most important section because it 'wraps everything up' into a neat package and conveys to the listener the power of your idea. Here you discuss the amount of money you are going to make, the scale of your idea, and the impact it is going to have on the market. What does the future look like? Why would someone invest? You outline about your goals and the potential for a bright future. You also let them know that there are risks, but that 'fortune favors the bold'. In the end, the listener must walk away with the idea that this is a once-in-a-lifetime opportunity and that YOU are the person to lead this effort.

In crafting your story, I recommend first writing each of the three sections above and then moving to a PowerPoint slide presentation in order to fully structure your thinking. Writing the narrative will allow you to think of how you want to tell your story, while putting together slides will give your story structure and flow. I have created an example in Appendix A to help you along. For this book I will use a simple business (a hair salon), but the process applies to almost any complex project or entrepreneurial endeavor.

Once you have your general story concept, it is time to create the presentation that will give your pitch structure and thoroughness. I suggest working with PowerPoint (or some other presentation software) because it is simple to use and encourages you to break down your thoughts into discreet slides.

The first step in creating a powerful presentation is to take the story you created above and organize it into sections that would make sense if seen on their own. For example, Radiance Salon might have the following general discussion areas:

1. The Idea
2. Market
3. Operations
4. Finances
5. Risks
6. Outcomes and what we want from you (closing)

Each of these sections will contain information that should already exist in your business plan, so you are simply organizing the information in a way that is easy to present.

Now that you have your general sections, you can create slides that follow the order you have laid out. I recommend no more than 20 slides for the entire presentation…which forces you to be very organized and brief! I have also found that the easiest way to create slides is to break down your story into a series of sentences that, when viewed in order, are both flowing and inclusive. For example, the sentences for a general presentation might look like this:

1. The Idea
    a. Slide 1: I have a great idea!
    b. Slide 2: The world needs this!
    c. Slide 3: The time is right!
2. The Market
    a. Slide 4: The market is huge
    b. Slide 5: People are attracted to it
    c. Slide 6: Competitors are not serving it well
3. Operations
    a. Slide 7: We will sell this in a compelling way
    b. Slide 8: It will look fantastic
    c. Slide 9: Customers will be served well
    d. Slide 10: Access to the product will be easy
    e. Slide 11: We will hire the best
4. Finances
    a. Slide 12: We assume certain things to be true
    b. Slide 13: Revenues will start slow and grow rapidly

      c.   Slide 14: There will be costs to start and operate the business

      d.   Slide 15: Profitability will occur soon and increase rapidly

      e.   Slide 16: Longer term the profits will be steady and significant

5.   Risks

      a.   Slide 17: There are risks that can be managed

6.   Outcomes and what we need from you

      a.   Slide 18: We want you as a partner and investor

      b.   Slide 19: We need $ _____

      c.   Slide 20: We are very excited about the future and want you to be a part of it!

As you may be able to tell, the pitch starts with excitement, goes through the details, and ends with excitement. In the middle of this 'arc' is the 'meat' of the presentation and thus contains the most slides. By writing the titles of the slides as sentences you should be able to literally read through the entire presentation in one long sentence. This gives your slides a cohesive feeling and lends to your credibility.

Once you have created this skeletal structure you then simply change the sentences to 3-4 word titles and populate the slides with relevant details...*in bullet form.* Each slide should have a short title and 5-6 bullets that support what you are trying to prove. The only exception is the financials, where you will likely place a spreadsheet or some other financial estimates. If you can use graphics, great, but don't rely on them unless they are backed up by hard data. Most investors are not fooled by glitz.

Now you have a slide presentation that will guide your story and allow you to get excited! Rules of thumb:

- **Short titles.** The titles of slides are simply a prompt to remind you what to say. The same goes for the bullet points. You should never just read the slides…the important thing is to memorize the story and use the slides as visual cues.

- **Limited bullets.** Never have more than 5-6 bullet points on any one slide. Nor should the bullets be long…no more than 7-8 words. You do not want your audience reading while you are speaking

- **Beware of promises.** In the financial section I always talk about 'goals' and 'plans'. You do not want to be promising returns you cannot guarantee.

- **Sections are not necessary**. I have included 1. The Idea, 2. The Market… etc because it is helpful for this example. If your slides are well put together and you speak with 'flow' then you will need very little external structure. A good story has an 'internal structure' that people will remember.

- **Reference supporting documents.** You should bring all the research that you conducted to create your plan, because not everything will go in the presentation. You can hand out price sheets, term sheets (addressed in a following section) and related articles. All this will allow you to answer questions on the fly and show that you have done your homework.

So now you have a plan, a presentation, and a 'pitch' that will wow investors. However this is still not enough and, in fact, is but a small part of the reason an investor will 'buy' what you are selling. In the next section I will discuss the central part of your offering, and it might not be what you think!

APPEALING TO THE HEART

The human mind likes to believe it is in charge. We think and ruminate, analyze and cogitate. But in the end, we act mainly from intuition and feeling. Our minds capture and organize, but our hearts decide. This is true whether we believe it or not, and so you must overcome your mind's resistance to this notion and learn how to offer your thoughts in a way that appeals to heart as much as the brain.

If you need more convincing, consider a couple of facts. First, conscious thought only represents about 5% of your mental processing (if that). The remaining 95% of your mental capacity is occupied processing the huge volume of data streaming in from your senses. If it were possible to consciously think about everything you experience you would end up frozen in place, overwhelmed by the complexity of the world. So your brain organizes the incoming data into two categories: That which to 'think' about, and that which can be handled in the background. Exactly how your brain sorts this data (which category it chooses for each bit of data) is dependent on your frame of reference (your stories, assumptions, choices). Whether you know it or not you *choose* that which you consciously process, and this choice determines your focus. Everything else is shunted to the background.

Second, the heart and stomach have almost as many nerve endings as the brain has neurons. Your stomach processes information in a way that is much like the unconscious brain. 'Gut feel' is a very powerful form of intuition. The heart is also constantly aware of and processing data from the external world. When other human beings (or anything living for that matter) enter your space your heart seeks to synchronize with them, and thus senses a 'vibe' about that person. In this way your heart knows as much about a situation as your brain.

Even more, your stomach, heart and brain are not discreet entities. Your entire body is a vibrating, resonating entity that is constantly in communication with the external world. Your conscious brain, that 5% of your mental processing, is merely a surface mechanism of a highly complex and acutely aware system. The human mind and body, taken together is an astounding piece of work!

This is important to your pitch because although your prospective investor may think she is going to make a logical decision, in actuality she is going to act from her 'gut' and then use the 5% of her conscious brain to *justify* the decision. Her entire body and unconscious mind has likely decided within 15 minutes of your entering the room! Her conscious mind is simply organizing your data to fit what she already believes in her heart. *So you must appeal to her heart as much as her mind.*

Our upbringing and schooling does not necessarily prepare us for this. In our schools 'science', which is simply a method of knowing the world, is revered. Logic is prized and strong arguments are valued. This is not bad, per se, it is simply a fact of our modern world. In learning to think logically, however, we have forgotten the art of 'creative appeal'. We have learned how to organize, but forgotten how to dance. We know how to calculate, but can't seem to paint. *Storytelling is not logical, it is inspirational.*

Inspiration is the feeling you get when you hear a beautiful piece of music, see a powerful work of art, or experience the magnificence of nature. Inspiration is, literally, the 'breath' of life and the way we connect to the living world. To inspire is to move the 95% of the mind and body that is operating in the background. This is the part that *decides*, and *so if you want to sell your idea you must inspire this part of your listener first.*

When you walk into the room your audience will immediately and unconsciously sense a number of things. First, they will sense whether you are certain or uncertain about your idea. If you feel confident about what you are presenting then your body language, facial expressions, and overall 'vibe' will cause their bodies to resonate with your own. *The audience will become confident with you.* Second, they will decide whether they 'like' you or not. To 'like' someone is to enjoy being in his or her presence. Generally,

19

happiness, joy and openness are 'attractive', while anger, tension, and closed-mindedness are 'repulsive'. If you can cultivate a happy countenance, your audience will likely be more attracted to what you are offering. *They will want to help you.*

Third, the people in the room will seek to relate to you. They will look at how you are dressed, the language you use and how you hold yourself. Each person will ask him or herself 'is this person someone I understand?' Behind this question lies something more fundamental: Trust. Your listener's body and subconscious mind are trying to figure out whether or not they are safe being around you, because in our tribal past this trust could mean our very survival. When we can relate to someone, and see how they are 'just like us', then we become more comfortable with the idea of trusting them.

Last, the audience will sense if you care about them...although they would likely never admit to this. Everyone wants to be recognized, respected and loved, and your listeners are no different. Human beings have developed, through evolutionary necessity, an acute sense of social inclusion or exclusion. To be cared for means to survive. To be left out means to die. Underneath your listener's analytical mind lies an emotional 'self' asking 'does he care about *me* and what *I* want?' If you can develop a genuine sense of care for the people you meet then you will exude this at a subconscious level, and they will respond. Their hearts will seek to synchronize with yours, and when they do they will feel your love.

In my experience it is the word 'love' that provokes the most discussion, doubt and misunderstanding. Love, in this context, is not the romantic love we see in movies and books but is instead an energy upon which all life is dependent. Love is connection. Love is a desire to unite with the light that lies behind all life. Love is God, and God is love. Love/God/Life are all the same energetically. When we connect to each other we affirm life itself, and in the process enter into the creative process. So when you walk into a room with confidence, joy, kindness and care you are resonating 'love' to everyone around you. You create an atmosphere in which the listeners will want to find a way to help you, because to help you is to help all life.

At this point you might be reeling a bit. This is likely *not* the business discussion you were expecting! But in my experience this is nonetheless how it works. Love what you are doing, love everyone in your life and love yourself…and others will find reasons to love you back. They will look at your plan and story with a predisposition to help. The logical 5% of your listener's minds will justify the decision they have already made in their hearts.

Your job is to create a 'state of heart' that attracts people and money to your endeavors. Here is how (in no particular order):

- **Do your research.** When you walk in the room you need to know your business, the audience, the competitors, *everything*. For every hour of time with your potential investors you should have done at least 100 hours of research. The time you dedicate to understanding your subject allows you to answer questions and objections, but more importantly it gives you a sense of confidence and 'knowing'. The strength you feel when you know your business will emanate from you like a beacon, and everyone in the room will resonate with you. They will know that YOU are the authority and will begin to trust your judgment.

- **Cultivate an optimistic countenance.** No matter what you hear or see, you stay strong in your beliefs. A little trick: Ask friends and family to throw objections at you, then stand there and say 'Good point, I believe we can do it anyway'. The key is not so much in your answer, but in your certainty in the face of doubt. Sometimes investors will pepper you with sarcastic and doubting comments *just to see how you will respond.* If you can't maintain optimism and faith in one meeting, then how can they trust you to stick with the idea in the face of *real* challenges? Your optimism and belief in yourself and your idea is your armor. You are bulletproof! When investors see that much self-assuredness, they almost always take a second look.

- **Smile.** For heaven's sake, make it look fun! You don't need to stand there smiling like a simpleton, but you can look people in the eye and show them happiness! Numerous studies have shown that when we smile at someone the brain of the recipient registers happiness. When people are happy they are more likely to be open to trusting and helping you. Be friendly, and at the very least smile when you say hello!

- **Dress appropriately.** Over the past 20 years there has been quite a change in the way entrepreneurs dress. It is not uncommon to see a 'creative tech genius' walk into a pitch wearing a torn flannel shirt, flip-flops and a nose ring (or five). I have no judgment on this at all - in fact it can be quite helpful with some investors. In the end, however, nobody wants this person as a CEO. You may be able to raise money in the 'grunge suit', but the first time you screw up or become difficult to manage you will be out…and many times without your shares. Savvy investors *always* build mechanisms into their share agreements to get rid of the entrepreneur if they need to. Don't plant that seed in their heads by looking like you just came from an Indie concert. An expensive suit isn't necessary, but try to look at least semi-professional.

- **Care.** When you genuinely care about the people around you, it shows in the way you carry yourself and the expression you have on your face. Human beings are biologically wired to distinguish between care and threat. Care means survival (especially to an infant), and threat can result in death. When you walk into the room you want to emanate the feeling that you are in this game as much for them as for yourself…and this should be *true*. If your investors do not do well then neither will you, so it is imperative that you truly do care about those who are about to entrust you with their money. I even suggest *telling them* you care, because when your words match your countenance then the resulting impact is doubly powerful.

- **Create a 'horse race'.** When you have multiple pitches on the same day or week, and have additional prospects in the hopper, then you will look and feel more confident. Speaking to only one investor will make you feel desperate for a 'yes', and it will show in how you handle yourself. Even if you don't have another pitch immediately lined up, you must deeply believe that you can and will get multiple investors interested. If an investor asks who else you are talking to, be prepared to rattle off a list of names. Investors are social beings...they all want to know that other people are 'with' them. Know the major investors in your industry and area.

- **Don't get caught up in NDA's.** Most savvy investors won't sign an NDA because they see hundreds of pitches and don't want to be restricted in what they say or do. If an investor *is* willing to sign an NDA, it does not mean much. They will talk anyway. And besides, your idea is not that important. 1% of a startup is the idea, 99% is the execution. So unless you have a plan to patent the next Post-it Note ®, don't fixate on your NDA. You can ask, but if they say no then go ahead and pitch anyway. Entrepreneurs who are obsessed with secrecy and ownership generally look insecure and naïve.

- **Set intentions.** It seems strange to me, but very few people actually set clear intentions before pitching an idea. Sure, they may have the general goal of getting investors interested, but rarely do entrepreneurs state what it is they are trying to achieve. If you want to come across as directed and effective, set an intention before you walk in the door and prior to presenting your idea. For instance, as you stand outside the meeting room you might say: My intention is to create excitement about this idea and then ask my listeners to invest. When in the meeting you might say to the group: My intention is to show you an exciting concept and then ask you to invest in the first stage. By being clear with yourself and your listeners you come across as a 'person on a mission', and are more likely to create resonance. When the intentions are unsaid or unclear you will appear uncertain and may not, for instance, actually remember to ask for money.

- **Be energetically 'you'.** The very best actors do not create powerful characters by putting on a mask…they create amazing performances *by channeling themselves through the role.* If the role calls for frustration, they find something that genuinely frustrates them and then use that emotion for the performance. For you this means finding something about your pitch that genuinely excites you, and then channeling that excitement through your words. If you try to fake excitement then your performance will fall flat. If excitement is not the first thing you feel, then find it through anger or frustration or joy or some other emotion. This is not to say I suggest going in to a pitch with an angry look on your face…but more to use anger as a vehicle for getting your energy up. The key is to find a place inside you that feel energized and then transmute that into excitement. Great leaders have done this throughout history, and you can do it too.

Some of these ideas may seem obvious, and to some extent they are, but the point is not to use them simply because they are smart things to do. The real reason to do these things is to create a sense of confidence and resonance *inside of you.* As I said earlier, your real power is subliminal. The things you actually say and do are merely vehicles for information. Your listeners will be much more affected by *how you are* than by what you say.

When you plan, craft your story, and create a heart-felt resonance inside of you, then you are 90% there. All you need to do to be fully prepared is practice, and that is the subject of the next chapter.

PRACTICE

There is an old proverb dating from the 1550's that declares, in Latin, 'Usos Promptos Facit.' Translated to English the phrase means 'Use Makes Perfect', which has evolved in modern times to 'Practice Makes Perfect'. In either case, the idea is that if we repeat an action over and over we will eventually create a 'perfect' representation of whatever it is we are seeking to do.

The idea of 'perfection' is, of course, a mental construct. In reality everything is perfect just the way it is…only we humans look upon the world and declare that it somehow needs to be better. Certainly we can create and build and hone, but the idea that our work improves the universe is a uniquely human conceit. Would you declare that a flower is 'imperfect' because it has not yet fully bloomed? Would you seek to improve the process of nature itself? Many men and women have tried, only to find that their efforts are meaningless (and sometimes destructive) in the grand scheme of things. *The perfection we seek lies in the process, not the outcome.*

When pitching your idea, then, the goal is not to practice until you are 'perfect' but to practice until you feel yourself in 'flow' with your topic. Practice is the process of becoming knowledgeable about and comfortable with what you are trying to do. When you do something over and over you begin to learn the intricacies of your subject. You see the little details that unpracticed minds might miss. Practice gives you a familiarity with your subject that allows you to 'riff' in the moment. When you have done something hundreds of times in hundreds of ways you come to know your topic so well that you can adapt to almost any circumstance.

Practice does not make you 'perfect', it makes you 'dynamic'.

As you repeat your pitch over and over it will move from the conscious part of your brain to the sub-conscious. The subconscious then handles the bulk of the processing in the background allowing your conscious mind to focus on other things, such as your listener's reactions to what you are saying. It is a lot like driving a car: When you first learn to drive you are focused on everything you need to do, but over time you relax and let your subconscious do the work. With your subconscious in charge the conscious mind can then focus on other things, such as what you are going to have for lunch or the conversation with your passengers. The mind is very good at multitasking once it becomes familiar with the content.

Practice, then, is imperative to delivering a dynamic and flowing pitch. The act of 'practicing', however, is not as easy as it might first seem. First, there are two types of practice:

1. Controlled Setting. This involves setting up a space, choosing your audience, and 'playing' with different approaches. Controlled practice allows you to test various approaches, get feedback, and make mistakes without consequence.

2. 'Real-world'. True to its name, this type of practice involves getting actual investor meetings and doing a complete pitch from beginning to end. Real-world practice is the most powerful because you get to experience an actual situation. It also, however, has direct consequences if the pitch does not go well.

Each type of practice has its benefits, and I recommend you do both. Generally you will want to have a number of 'controlled' practices before setting up 'real-world' pitches. When you decide to go out and pitch for real I suggest you choose lower-consequence pitches first, such as low probability investors or investors who will be inherently friendly to your cause. This approach allows you to practice 'for real' without the threat of losing a high value investor.

Second, there are different exercises you can use to practice a pitch. Over the years I have developed methods that, when practiced diligently and repeatedly, result in a very confident style. Most need to be conducted in a controlled setting, but some can be applied in real-world situations (and indeed in many cases an investor will force it!):

- **Titles only.** Copy your slides into a new file, then remove all the content on each slide except for the title. Open this new presentation and run through your pitch very rapidly using only ONE SENTENCE to describe each slide. This process forces you to summarize your presentation and highlights any 'flow' issues. You should be able to run through your entire pitch in less than 5 min and still have it make sense. Practicing this way gives you the confidence to tell your story quickly and fluidly…and prepares you for when an investor inevitably tells you to 'hurry it up'.

- **Backwards.** Start at the end of your slides and do the presentation in reverse. This can be done with 'titles only', or with the full slides (I recommend doing both). Starting at the conclusion forces your brain to deal with the content independent of context, which improves both your memory and your understanding of the flow of the document.

- **Random slide.** Set up a projector, stand at the front of the room and ask someone choose a slide at random. Talk to the slide, giving it brief context so that the listener understands where it 'sits' in the flow of the presentation. Do this until you have spoken to each slide. This type of practice reinforces your understanding of the purpose each slide occupies in the whole, and gives you the confidence to address any topic at random.

- **One look.** Project your presentation on a wall, but only allow yourself one look at each slide. Briefly glance at the content and then speak as if the slide were not there. This can actually be quite difficult because by now you will have become used to having the information readily available. As you do this over and over you will eventually become so familiar with your slides that you will be able to speak and listen at the same time, which is key to handling a dynamic room.

- **Interrupted questions.** Set up a room with a friendly group of people as an audience. Ask them to interrupt your presentation with questions. Have fun with this! As you become more confident, ask them to become more obnoxious and demanding. Over time you will find yourself able to relax and handle highly uncertain situations. Your knowledge and flow will shine through and you will gain the respect of even the most hard-nosed investors.

- **No slides.** Stand up and deliver your entire pitch without slides. This is difficult, but can be the most powerful way to pitch because slides can actually detract from the energy of your message. The very best pitch artists sometimes use very little supporting information, instead relying on their knowledge and charisma to make points. This method of practice also prepares you for the day when you either lose your slides or find out that there is no way to project your presentation. Be prepared to talk anytime, anywhere!

- **Self talk.** This practice is both odd and powerful, because it involves storytelling within your own mind. Most human thoughts take the form of stories because this is the way the brain most efficiently and effectively both remembers and processes information. If you can think through your pitch as if you were telling yourself a story you will more easily remember and resonate with the information. I suggest you go for a walk and talk through your pitch as if you were explaining your idea to an imaginary friend. Tell the story of your idea out loud and silently. Through this process you will become more comfortable with yourself and the flow of your thoughts.

If you were to try each of these methods you would be forced to practice at least 20-30 hours, and this would make a huge difference in both your ability and confidence. The more you do it the better you will become, and the better you become the more your energy will become 'attractive'.

As you go through your practice, keep in mind these rules of thumb:

- **There is no such thing as 'perfection'.** The whole idea of perfection is a mental construct that we use to whip ourselves to perform. Holding yourself to an impossible goal and criticizing everything you do only results in stress and worry, which is felt by your listeners. You are, in fact, 'perfect' in every moment because you are doing your best. Let go of self-abuse and focus on learning and growth. Get a little better with every pitch and eventually you will become a master. Not *perfect*, but a *master*.

- **Ask for support.** Don't fall into the 'lone wolf' trap by thinking that asking for support equals weakness. The smartest and most courageous thing you can do is to reach out to others for assistance. Find people who have experience pitching investors and ask them for advice. Get a mentor. Ask your friends and family to help you practice. Hire a coach. *Reach out.* As you connect to others you will find strength and encouragement.

- **Get feedback.** Most of us avoid getting feedback because we don't want to hear what is 'wrong' with us or the things we are saying. We want to hear nothing but unconditional positive regard. This is natural, but it is also extremely limiting because we miss out on valid, helpful input from people with different perspectives. For this reason it is imperative that you de-personalize your pitch. Your work is *not a reflection of your worth.* Feedback is merely the process of seeking wider perspectives, not a weapon meant to diminish you. Be courageous and purposefully seek out people who will *not* agree with you. Ask for honesty and constructive criticism. Learning to hear honest feedback not only helps you achieve, but it also gives you the strength to weather the occasionally brutal honesty that investors, and your customers, are known to give.

- **Iterate**. As you practice, get feedback, and improve, your pitch is naturally going to change. The content, structure, tone and emphasis points will shift as you learn what works and what falls flat. For this reason you must be willing to make modifications. Your pitch will never be the same from one meeting to the next, so try to see your materials as fluid. After each practice session and pitch try to 'tweak' the slides and approach to make it a bit better.

- **Make mistakes**. The best way to learn is to purposefully make mistakes. 'Failure' is, in my book, one of the greatest teachers. Take risks. Try different approaches. Do something unconventional. Jump around the room. Loosen yourself up. As you try new things you will learn what works and what does not work. Your confidence will increase as you see that there is nothing to fear. Some of the greatest pitch-men (and women) of all times were those who did something unconventional. Be aggressive and seek to fail!

- **Laugh**. In the end, most of us fear 'looking stupid' or being ridiculed for who we are and what we say. This starts in childhood when our parents or peers laugh at us when we are trying to express ourselves. So we shut down. We have dreams of being humiliated (ie standing in public naked), and live in fear of being the focus of derision. The problem is that while the feeling of fear is real, the consequences of 'looking stupid' are *not*. Nothing is going to happen to you if you say something 'wrong' or out of place. You are not going to die. Learn to laugh at yourself! Have fun as you practice! Allow yourself to be human! You will find that, over time, your fear will diminish and your energy will increase. People will laugh *with* you not *at* you. Your confidence and charisma will become infectious. Laugh, smile and have fun!

In sum, the more you practice the better you will become. Each time you deliver your pitch you will become a little bit more comfortable and clear. Over the long term you will develop the ability to tailor your content 'on the fly' to match your listener's moods and interests. You will start to think less about your pitch and more about what the investor wants, and this is the key to raising money. In reality, the investor is evaluating your idea on a whole different level, which is the subject of the next section.

APPROACHING INVESTORS

Fortunately for the aspiring entrepreneur, there are many people and organizations in this world that possess financial capital (money). And even better, the vast majority of those people are interested in making a return on that money. So you will have plenty of people to whom you can 'pitch' your idea. For many new entrepreneurs this over-abundance of targets creates a 'spray and pray' approach whereby the founders talk endlessly to anyone who will listen and treat all dollars as exactly the same. This method may result in getting the funds you want (if only because you have talked to so many people) but it can also bring unwanted or unhelpful investors into your world.

There are many ways to evaluate investors, and I am going to help you by offering some thoughts from mistakes that I have made along the way. First and foremost, an investor can be 'dumb money' or 'smart money' (see also the definitions links in Appendix F). Dumb money comes from an investor that is not in the business of funding startups. This is not so much a judgment as a realistic assessment of what the investor knows or can do for you. Your parents, friends and recently-wealthy acquaintances are many times 'dumb money' because they are investing rather blindly. They know you and like you and will likely not read the documents or plans you provide, nor will they tend to negotiate on the terms of the deal. This investor can also be called 'easy money', or 'friends and family'. Again, this does not mean your parents or friends are stupid. All I mean is that this money is likely not going to get you introductions to potential customers, large investors, or have contacts in key places. The people are not 'dumb', but the money is.

Smart money comes from investors who know startups, understand the industry you occupy, have contacts in the investment world, and who are willing to help you become successful. With smart money comes access, support and knowledge....benefits that dumb money cannot provide. Smart money investors will also, however, be tough negotiators because they know what can happen down the road. They will want terms that lock you up and guarantee their success as much as possible. When you choose a 'smart money' investor you are able to leverage much more than their wallet, but you will pay for that access through a more stringent term sheet.

Given my terminology, you might be tempted to think that smart money is good and dumb money is bad. Yet this is not the case. Dumb money can be very helpful and important at the seed stage of an investment because the investors are willing to take a leap of faith and not be sticklers on ownership. They will trust that you know what you are doing. This places a great deal of responsibility on your part, however, because in later rounds the 'smart' investors will do everything they can to 'cram down', or dilute, the earlier rounds. Friends and family can be sitting ducks for a savvy Venture Capitalist who knows how to cut a good deal.

This brings me to the second consideration about investors: Ethics. Not all investors are caring people. Some of them will do whatever they can to steal your company, especially if you struggle or find yourself in a cash crunch. When speaking with a potential investor make sure to look into their background. Talk to people who have dealt with them in the past. Were they trustworthy? Are they helpful? How did they act when things did not look good? I have personally dealt with all types, from investors who were incredibly caring and supportive in tough times to those who called me every day to scream at me and threaten my job. Even though you may be tempted to take investment from anyone who offers it, you will want to choose only those who you like and trust.

Third, the type of investor you choose will depend on the round of investment and the amount you are seeking. Generally, various rounds and investor types flow as follows:

1. Startup. These are the first dollars that create the company. If, for example, I want to incorporate a company with 2,000,000 shares of stock with a par value (starting value) of

$.001 per share (a tenth of a cent), then I will put $2,000 into the company. This initial funding comes from the founder.

2. Seed. This is the money that allows you to create the first prototypes, mock-ups or plans. It is also called 'friends and family', 'self-funding' or 'seed capital', and can be anywhere from $10,000 to $100,000. Because the company is so new, the share price will be low…but will have increased from the previous round (See Appendix D for a sample Cap Table). Investors in this round can be yourself, your family, and/or your friends. In this round it is fine to have 'dumb money' because you are simply looking to get things off the ground. Keep in mind, however, that you have a responsibility to this money and will need to protect these people as you negotiate later rounds.

3. Angel. This round is slightly larger than seed capital and can range from $100,000 to $2,000,000. Angel investors can be either smart or dumb money, depending on their qualifications (there is a legal term called a 'qualified investor' that is defined below. Here I am not referring to legal qualification as per SEC rules, but more to the level of understanding about your industry and startups generally). If you feel very confident in your plan and understand the investment world very well, then it is OK to seek 'dumb angel' money, perhaps from a single wealthy investor. Most angels, however, are 'smart' money and will have lawyers, processes and requirements. In the US there are many, many

individual angels and almost as many groups of wealthy people who have created 'Angel Groups' that target this level of investment.

4. Round 1. Also knows as 'Series A' or 'Series A preferred' (the 'preferred referring to the type of stock). Investors at this level typically 'come in' at anywhere from $2,000,000 to $6,000,000. If your first round is fairly large, say $6,000,000, then you may see a consortium of investors form where each takes a portion of the total 'book'. If there are three investors, for example, then two of them may take $1,500,000 while the third 'leads' the round by taking $3,000,000. The 'lead' investor will likely want a board seat and will represent the other members of the consortium (for the most part). Investors in this type of round are typically Venture Capitalists (VC's), venture arms of large corporations,

5. Round 2. Theoretically these numbered rounds can go on indefinitely, but eventually a company would go to the public markets because the figures involved get prohibitively high. Investors in the second round are typically larger VCs who look to place between $5,000,000 and $10,000,000 per investor. This round might typically hold 3-8 investors with a total investment of anywhere from $10,000,000 to $100,000,000. In these larger, later rounds your company will have built significant market share. You would likely be looking to expand overseas, buy a competitor, or some other such strategic move. These later rounds will have different

preferred stock 'tranches' with different pricing and rights. Each round will have its own designation, such as Series A-1 preferred, Series B preferred, Series B-1 preferred, etc. If you are seeking this level of investment, you are likely not going to need this part of the book because you will have lawyers and bankers doing this work for you!

6. Strategic. A strategic round can happen at any point along the way, but usually occurs later in the process. A strategic investor is many times a large company that wants to have access to your technology or establish a longer term working relationship. The money at this level is usually between $2,000,000 to $5,000,000, but it could be more or less depending on the company and the arrangement. Strategic investors would likely have their own round because of the special circumstances around the deal. It is not uncommon for this round to be a Series A-1 or 2 because the rights of the stock might be the same as Series A, the round being a simple 'add-on' to the earlier book of investors.

7. Public. This is the ultimate round of external investment because it involves very large sums of money (usually) and can generate the most change within a company. In short, this is simply the process of selling shares to the general public instead of to private investors. Having your shares listed on a public exchange makes them more 'liquid' (sellable), but it also completely changes the nature of the company. Taking a company from a privately financed

company to a public entity is a process that would require a book in-and-by itself. Suffice it to say, if you have reached this point prepare yourself for some exciting times!

As you can see, the capitalist system has created a number of ways to fund your business. You have an array of people and institutions that are designed to provide capital at each step of your growth. Your job is to maximize your appeal and then choose wisely. Investors in the early rounds can help you find larger investors in the later rounds. Some investors are sharks, while others are angels. It is up to you to select those that you like, that you trust and who have experience in what you are trying to build. A good investor can make your business…but a bad investor can break it.

Overall, think carefully about how much money you need and the type of person/institution with whom you want to create a relationship. Ask for enough money to take you to the next level, but not so much as to give away too much ownership in the company. If at all possible, you want to maintain 51% control as long as possible (as shown in Appendix D). As to the type of investor, I recommend writing out the attributes you would like to see in a person and then ask each investor very pointed questions. How do they react in a crisis? What are their values? Beliefs? Will they respect and support you? If you can become good at this you will choose people who can help you become very successful!

Once you have spoken to a lot of investors you will see that some are interested and others are not. This is good. You want to narrow down your pool to only those who believe in your idea and support you as a leader. This smaller group will likely signal interest by sending you a term sheet that has been generated by their lawyers. This is the opening of the negotiation phase, and is the subject of the next chapter.

THE NEGOTIATION

If you educate yourself well, build a solid plan, prepare a compelling story, and appeal to the heart of the listener, then you will have maximized your chances of securing funds. The rest is up to the investor. At this point, then, you must begin to think like an investor, because as you extol the virtues and possibilities of your idea, the investors listening to your pitch will be asking themselves a number of important questions related the viability and potential return of what you are pitching. Some of these questions include:

1. Is this a good idea?
2. Is it the right time for this idea?
3. Is it a good plan?
4. Is this the right person or team to execute on the plan?
5. How much money will they need?
6. How much of the business can I get for my investment?
7. Does this business fit into my portfolio of investments?
8. Who would be a potential buyer for this company?

9. What is the likely return on my investment if it sells?

A smart investor (see definitions of 'smart money' vs. 'dumb money' in Appendix F) will seek to answer these questions by 'testing' your idea through objection. This is why I stress not to take criticism personally, because investors are simply doing their job when they raise doubts about you, your team, your plan and your business. They are doing what is called 'due diligence' by digging into your assumptions and questioning your plan. Your ability to anticipate and answer these questions with confidence and clarity will go a long way to convince an investor to join your team.

During this due diligence there is another, more subtle process going on in the background as well. As investors pick apart you and your premise/story/facts /assumptions they are also seeking to diminish your price. If they can make you feel insecure about your idea and prospects for raising money, then they will be able to secure a better deal. This is why you *must not* take anything personally. Everything that happens in the pitch is a form of negotiation. The stronger you appear, the better your position.

Here are a few ways an investor, especially a venture capitalist, will seek to negotiate:

- Diminish the idea. A smart investor wants you to question yourself. If you do, he/she can question how you have valued the company (see 'valuation' below).

- Delay. An investor tries to get you excited with vague promises and then strings you along for months in the hopes that you become desperate. The more worried and frustrated they can make you, the higher the likelihood they can get good terms.

- Demand exclusivity. Investors will sometimes ask that they be the only one to look at your opportunity. This is also to create desperation. If they are the only potential investor then eventually you will have to beg them for money.

To counter these tactics, you can do a number of things both during and after the pitch:

- Stay confident. Never take anything personally. Be determined to make your idea successful, while at the same time listening with an ear toward making your idea better. Objections can help you improve your idea and pitch. Listen with a curious ear!

- Set time frames. It takes at least 4-6 months to raise money, so you must ensure that you have the resources to see the process through. Set goals and dates, and tell each potential investor up front that you will not make any changes. It takes guts to do this, especially when investors are not beating down your door, but it is important because it shows confidence. *You must control the process.*

- Create a horse race. As I said earlier, always speak with more than one investor. If an investor gets the idea that they are your only prospect, they will know that they have all the power in the negotiation. Many times an investor will ask 'who else are you talking to?' Your answer should be immediate and either mention specific people/firms or let the listener know that there are at least 2 other parties involved in the process.

If the investor is truly interested in your idea, then he/she will request that you provide a 'term sheet' (see the example in Appendix E). A term sheet is simply a document that specifies the terms under which you are willing to sell your shares. Your term sheet is the beginning of your negotiation, so you want to make sure that you ask for what you want. An early money investor such as a 'seed' (friends and family, etc) will rarely negotiate on a term sheet because they do not understand the business. An experienced investor, however, will almost always ask for special terms and conditions that give them preferences upon sale, liquidation, etc.

Areas of term sheet negotiation include:

- Price. This is the most common negotiation point because it represents how much of the company an investor can get for their money. A common investor question is 'what is your pre-money valuation?' This question is about price because the value you place on the company will determine the number of shares they can get for each dollar they invest. If you value your company at $1,000,000, for example, then an investment of $100,000 will buy 10% of your enterprise. If the investor can negotiate your valuation down to $500,000 (by diminishing your confidence, idea, or value), then they will get 20% of your company for the same $100,000. For more on valuing your company and calculating share ownership, see Appendix D.

- Liquidation preference. When a company sells, each of the investors is paid for their shares according to the number of shares they hold. If an investor buys your shares at $1 each, and the company sells for $10 per share, then the investor pockets a profit of $9 per share. But if the company sells for only $1.10 per share, then the investor only makes $.10 per share profit. In order to mitigate this risk, a smart investor will ask for a 'liquidation preference' that specifies that they make at least ____ return before anyone else makes money. For example, an investor may ask for a 3x liquidation preference. This says that they will make 3 times their money before anyone else gets a dime. If your company sells for $3 per share or higher, then everyone gets equal money. If, however, the company sells for less than $3, then nobody gets paid anything until that investor gets at least 3 times his or her money. You may negotiate this down to a 2x or even a 1.5x liquidation preference, depending on the strength of your position. It is important to negotiate this point because, upon sale, it could mean the difference between you making something…or nothing at all.

- Voting rights. Everything in a company is about *control*. If you control the decision making process, then you can direct the future of the company. You can pick the board, the officers, the sale price, virtually everything. Your control comes from your vote, and your vote comes from your shares. Most companies are organized to have one vote per each share of the company. When you start the company you will have 100% of the votes because you own all the shares. As you sell shares to an investor, however, you will then begin to give away some of your votes to outside parties (Appendix D shows how this happens). If an investor gets 51% of the company's voting shares, then they can do anything they want…including get rid of you. An investor will therefore be constantly trying to increase his/her voting shares during the negotiation. One way to do this is to create different 'classes' of shares, whereby some shares are voting shares and some are not. This way they can maximize their power in the company by, say, insisting that other types of investors be given non-voting shares. With preferable voting rights an investor maximizes his or her power position in the company.

- Board seats. If your company is a corporation (as opposed to a partnership) then you must have a Board of Directors. A Board determines the governance of the company (i.e. officers and other directors), approves additional shares for sale, and generally oversees the direction and strategy of the operation. A Board is responsible to the shareholders and always seeks to maximize shareholder value. If your investor becomes a major shareholder, then, it makes sense that they would want to put someone on the Board that represents them. A smart investor will push to get someone on the board, but you want to be VERY careful who gets a seat. Once someone is on the Board they are hard to remove, and when a board member votes it is usually in their shareholder's interest. So if you give away too many board seats you will be left as a minority on votes that could impact your role at the company. Board seats are very valuable, so you must use them to your advantage.

There are many other terms that may be included in a term sheet, and I highly suggest you contact a startup lawyer in order to familiarize yourself with the various areas of negotiation. Some of these terms may or may not include:

- Founder's salaries (the acceptable salary range for the founders)
- Option pool (the number of stock options available for employees or partners)
- Founder vesting (asking the founders to activate their shares over a period of years so that the investors are assured that the founders will stick with it)

- Pro-rata rights (allowing existing investors to put in money with future investors in order to keep their existing % ownership)

Each round of investment will have different terms because the valuation will change (increase, hopefully!) and the investors will have different interests. As you become more successful your negotiating position will strengthen, and you will likely have more access to money. In the beginning, however, it is crucial that you come across as confident and knowledgeable. Potential investors are more willing to give on certain points in the negotiation if they believe that your idea can make them a lot of money and that you are the one to make your business successful. Remember: *If their heart is sold, then their minds will make the necessary adjustments to make it work.*

CONCLUSION

I have discussed quite a few topics in this book, so a brief review is in order. First, it is important to understand your power as a creative human being. Your thoughts and ideas are incredibly powerful if you can learn to bring them into the world in a compelling way. Your ability to do this depends on your skill as a storyteller. Second, in order to be able to tell a powerful story you must have thought through your topic thoroughly and completely. You do this by creating a business plan. Third, to convince others of the viability of your idea and plan, you will need to tell a story that people can both understand and to which they can relate. Human beings have been telling each other stories for thousands of years, so you must make your investment 'pitch' a story of heroic proportions!

Fourth, people 'buy' a story when they feel good about it, and most of us feel through our heart. You must learn to appeal to the heart and soul of your listeners. Help them feel your excitement and your intentions. Fifth, in order to tell your story with flow and heart you will need to practice…over and over and over and….over. Practice in different settings and with different approaches. As you practice you will experience perfection. Sixth, seek investors who match your needs, values and beliefs. Talk to anyone who will listen, but choose those who will not only fund you but support you with contacts, emotional encouragement and expertise. Lastly, negotiate with an understanding of what your investors are trying to achieve. Seek to create win-wins so that everyone can make money in a way that is resonant to each party.

Securing investors for your business is, like all sales, a numbers game. A certain number of investors will be interested in your idea, and a fraction of those will be willing to invest. An even smaller fraction will be 'right' for you. The reality of this math makes it imperative that you talk to a lot of people and groups. Of every 20 people you approach, only 3-4 may be interested. Of those, only 1 may be serious…and this person may not be right. The only way to get a strong, supportive group of investors is to be patient, talk to a lot of people, and believe that your partner/investor is waiting to be found. This process is not unlike finding a mate, so *don't settle*. Ask for what you want and believe that you can get it!

Most importantly, I ask you to go into this process with a 'learning orientation to life'. Being rejected is an important part of this process, and it is not personal. You are a valuable human being worthy of happiness and love. Never doubt that, no matter what you might hear. Use this process to become tougher, smarter and greater as a human being. If you can do this then there is no way to 'lose' anything! You will only gain. So keep going, keep the faith, and believe in your ability to create! I believe in you!

APPENDIX A: RADIANCE SALON STORY ARC

I have chosen a small hair salon as an example because it is uncomplicated and relatively easy for everyone to understand. The purpose of these examples is to show you the phrasing, structure and tone of business communication. Your own business or idea will undoubtedly have a different feel but should take on the same general structure.

Radiance Salon

1. **The idea and its origin.** I grew up in this town and know intimately the people and the area. I have a very large network of friends, and lots of people for whom I cut hair. People trust me and like me. One afternoon I was walking down main street and saw that there was a space available for rent. I immediately realized that there were NO hair salons on main street, most of them being at the mall 5 miles away. I sat and observed the foot traffic and saw that approximately

30 people per hour walked by the space, and that many of them were women. When I went home I did a quick analysis of the population and the number of local salons and came to the conclusion that a new salon would do very well in this location. I am extremely excited to create a profitable new business in this area!

2. **Making the idea a reality.** My plan is to rent the space, buy used equipment from a salon going out of business in the next town, and begin to market myself for a grand opening in October. I will create a 'buzz' about my opening by holding 'hair parties' at various women's houses around town over the next few months. At these events I will give free haircuts and then hand out coupons to drive traffic to the salon once it opens. I will also place business cards under windshields, place flyers with local merchants (dry cleaners, Laundromats, dentists, etc). During the space build-out I will be creating a web-site where people can make appointments, and I will put up a Facebook page to which I will direct my 650 friends. In the beginning I will hire one mani/pedi person and one other stylist. Ultimately I plan to expand to up to 3 mani/pedi providers and 6 stylists. I will differentiate myself from my competitors by 1) providing amazing service…with kindness, 2) hiring experienced stylists with strong backgrounds, and 3) using my large network to integrate into the community. My knowledge of the salon business, background and community contacts make me uniquely qualified to run a successful salon!

I simply need $20,000 to get started, and this is where YOU come in!

3. **A vision of a powerful outcome.** As with any new venture there are risks, and this is no exception.* My network may not prove to back me, the location may not draw as many people as I think, and I might not be able to get the stylists I need. But I believe these risks to be minimal and have come up with contingency plans for all of them. In the end, an investor who backs me will be backing an experienced, local hair stylist who is determined to succeed. When my salon is up and running I believe that it will generate a positive cash flow of at least $5,000 per month, of which you, as an investor, will receive a portion. This number could go as high as $15,000 per month. In addition you would receive an ownership stake in an enterprise that, if sold, could be worth in excess of $100,000. You have an opportunity to become involved in a very profitable business…and participate in a local business enterprise that will employ local citizens!

You may find yourself hesitating when discussing risks, but investors will appreciate your candor and see this as a sign that you have truly thought through everything

APPENDIX B: RADIANCE SALON SLIDE PRESENTATION STRUCTURE

In order to create a solid presentation I have broken down the Radiance story into the 6 main sections of the business plan, and then dedicated anywhere from 1-5 slides to each section. Each slide will have a title at the top of the page as indicated below. You should be able to read through the titles very quickly and tell a story from the top level. This high level flow is the key to a good presentation. If your story does not make sense at this level then you must play with the slide order and titles until it does.

1. The Idea
    a. Slide 1: A high-end hair salon for our town
    b. Slide 2: The market is underserved in this area
    c. Slide 3: Foot traffic is high
2. The Market
    a. Slide 4: The market is large and growing
    b. Slide 5: The demographics are young and trendy

     c.   Slide 6: Competitors are scarce and distant

3. Operations

     a.   Slide 7: We will market through networks

     b.   Slide 8: The design will be attractive

     c.   Slide 9: Service will be paramount

     d.   Slide 10: The web site will be friendly and accessible

     e.   Slide 11: Hiring will be critical and selective

4. Finances

     a.   Slide 12: Pricing, volume and customer retention assumptions

     b.   Slide 13: Revenues will start slow and grow rapidly

     c.   Slide 14: Costs of starting is significant but operating costs low

     d.   Slide 15: Profitability will occur in the 9th month, and rise rapidly

     e.   Slide 16: By year 3 the profits will be steady and significant

5. Risks

     a.   Slide 17: The risks are low but need to be recognized

6. Outcomes and what we need from you

     a.   Slide 18: We are looking for investors who want to be partners in a local business

     b.   Slide 19: We need $30,000 for the initial build and expect to distribute $2,000 per month by year 3, not including capital value

c. Slide 20: We are excited to have you on board! Any questions?

APPENDIX C: RADIANCE SALON PRESENTATION CONTENT

Once you have the high-level presentation structure you can then begin to populate your slides. For this example I have added bullet-points to each slide. Your bullets should always be very short and easy to read. Remember, your slide content is simply a reminder and a prompt for what you are going to say. You do not want your listener focused on reading your slides…you want them listening to *you*. In some cases you won't have any words at all, but instead will have an image or chart of some kind.

1. The Idea
    a. Slide 1: A High-End Hair Salon and Spa
        - Cutting edge style
        - Range of services
        - Fantastic location
        - Impeccable customer service
        - Community focused

    b.   Slide 2: An Underserved Market

- Map of all hair salons and barbershops

    c.   Slide 3: High Foot Traffic

- Chart showing foot traffic by time of day

2.   The Market

    a.   Slide 4: The Market

- Population projections: 50,000 now to 75,000 in 5 years
- City center is becoming popular
- Haircuts are a staple of life
- Mani/Pedicures are status symbols and social experiences

    b.   Slide 5: Demographics

- Average age of city center is dropping
- Young people are looking for 'big-city style'
- Cafés and trendy restaurants are opening
- Yoga and pilates are increasingly popular

    c.   Slide 6: Competitors

- Most competitors are 'old school' AND
- Are located in mall 5 miles away
- For the population there are not enough shops
- Competitor visits show poor customer service

3. Operations

    a. Slide 7: Marketing

        • Personal networks

        • Group gatherings

        • Flyers and advertisements

        • Partnerships with local merchants

    b. Slide 8: Design

        • Mocked-up designs/pictures of storefront and inside

    c. Slide 9: Customer Service Imperative

        • Door greeting

        • Beverages

        • Scalp massage

        • Birthday and special occasion emails

        • Detailed customer records

        • Kindness and listening above all

    d. Slide 10: Web Presence

        • Mock-up of site

        • Tour of planned functions

    e. Slide 11: Hiring Critical

        • Experienced

        • Educated

        • Stylish

        • Reliable

        • 'Good People'

4. Finances

    a. Slide 12: Assumptions

- Pricing (see handout of services and prices)
- Volume (Assumed 10% market share and bi-monthly visits)
- Customer Retention (75%)
- Male/Female/Child Ratio (30/60/10)

    b. Slide 13: Revenues

- Chart of revenue calculations over time based on assumptions

    c. Slide 14: Costs

- Chart of startup and ongoing costs by year

    d. Slide 15: Profitability in 9th Month

- Spreadsheet showing Revenue-Costs for first two years

    e. Slide 16: By year 3 the profits will be steady and significant

- Spreadsheet showing Revenue-Costs for 5 year period

5. Risks

    a. Slide 17: Risks

- New competitors
- Traffic not what expected
- Costs increase
- Customers unhappy

6. Outcomes and what we need from you

    a. Slide 18: Investors Wanted!

- Local
- Easy to work with
- Interested in long-term potential
- Believe in us

    b. Slide 19: Needs and potential returns

- $30,000 to get up and running
- Upon profitability, cash returns will be distributed monthly
- Goal is $2,000 per month by year 3
- Capital value will be returned upon sale

    c. Slide 20: Join Us!

- Generate local jobs
- Build community
- Create beauty!
- Make money!

K.C. HILDRETH

APPENDIX D: SAMPLE CAPITALIZATION TABLE

At each stage in your company's existence you will have an ownership structure. If you are a small 'sole proprietorship' then you will likely own 100%. If you are a partnership then it may be 50-50%. If you are a corporation then the ownership structure can become more complex. Ownership structure is represented by what is called a 'capitalization table', or a 'cap table' for short. A cap table is simply a list of the owners of the company, the number of shares each owns, the type of shares (the rights and preferences), and the percentage of the company each ownership stake represents.

In this appendix I am including a sample cap table (on the right) and the calculation that went into the fund raising round (on the left). I have chosen to exclude the types of shares in each round in order to make the example more readable. This is an actual example from a company I helped fund some years ago.

When this company was founded the initial owners put $10,000 into the company at $.001 per share. There were 10,000,000 shares sold out of a total of 20,000,000 authorized. The founders therefore owned 100% of the shares outstanding (if you have trouble reading any of these tables or would like a free template, please go to: www.kchildreth.com/freedownloads):

Stage 1: Founding		
Pre-money valuation	$	10,000
Price per share	$	0.001
Shares offered		10,000,000
Money raised	$	**10,000**
Total shares outstanding		10,000,000
Post-money valuation	$	10,000

Ownership	Shares	%	Control
Founder 1	5,500,000	55%	
Founder 2	2,000,000	20%	**100%**
Founder 3	2,500,000	25%	
Total Issued Shares	10,000,000	100%	
Authorized shares remaining	10,000,000		

Shareholder	Shares	% Owned
Founder 1	5,500,000	55.00%
Founder 2	2,000,000	20.00%
Founder 3	2,500,000	25.00%
	10,000,000	100%

Because $10,000 was not enough to build a prototype necessary to raise further funds, the owners decided to raise $100,000 from two friends of the founders. In this round the company had already been formed and a lot of business plan work done, so the price per share was raised from $.001 per share to $.10 per share (reflecting an increase in the value of the company from $10,000 to $1,000,000. The new 'angels' bought 9% of the company with their $100,000, leaving the founders with 91% of the shares (still in control):

Stage 2: Early Angel		
Pre-money valuation	$	1,000,000
Price per share	$	0.10
Shares offered		1,000,000
Money raised	**$**	**100,000**
Total shares outstanding		11,000,000
Post-money valuation	$	1,100,000

Ownership	Shares	%	Control
Founder 1	5,500,000	50%	
Founder 2	2,000,000	18%	**91%**
Founder 3	2,500,000	23%	
Early Angel	1,000,000	9%	
Total outstanding	11,000,000	100%	
Authorized shares remaining	9,000,000		

Shareholder	Shares	% Owned
Founder 1	5,500,000	50.00%
Founder 2	2,000,000	18.00%
Founder 3	2,500,000	23.00%
Angel 1	500,000	4.50%
Angel 2	500,000	4.50%
	11,000,000	100%

With the prototype built, the founders now wanted to raise a larger amount of money to build the first market-ready version of their technology. They raised $540,000 from three angel investors and sold approximately 9% more of the company. Because the prototype had been finished and the plan finalized, the price per share went up to $.50, so the founders could get more money for the 9% of the company they had to sell. In the previous round they only got $100,000 for 9% of the company. This time around they got $540,000. You will notice, also, that the other shareholders are 'diluted' because they did not participate in this round and ended up owning less of the company. When outside parties buy stock then the existing shareholders must either buy enough shares to keep up their percentage of ownership or accept that their ownership stake will be diluted. A VC will negotiate 'pro-rata' rights to ensure that they are allowed to buy more shares (and keep their ownership stake) if another investor gets involved:

Stage 3: Angel

Pre-money valuation	$	5,500,000
Price per share	$	0.50
Shares offered		1,080,000
Money raised	$	**540,000**
Total shares outstanding		12,080,000
Post-money valuation	$	6,040,000

Ownership	Shares	%	Control
Founder 1	5,500,000	46%	
Founder 2	2,000,000	17%	83%
Founder 3	2,500,000	21%	
Early Angel	1,000,000	8%	
Angel	1,080,000	9%	
Total outstanding	12,080,000	100%	
Authorized shares remaining	7,920,000		

Shareholder	Shares	% Owned
Founder 1	5,500,000	45.68%
Founder 2	2,000,000	16.61%
Founder 3	2,500,000	20.76%
Early Angel 1	500,000	4.15%
Early Angel 2	500,000	4.15%
Angel 1	400,000	3.32%
Angel 2	400,000	3.32%
Angel 3	240,000	1.99%
	12,040,000	100%

Now that there is a working model in the market, the board wanted to get a larger round for marketing, hiring and operational expansion. This round sought approximately $5,000,000 from two VC's who participated equally. The share price increased to $.75, and the founders were diluted down to 52% ownership (which is good, because it is sometimes hard to maintain control when a VC invests). Post-money the company is now valued at $14,215,232, and almost all of the shares outstanding have been sold:

Stage 4: First Round VC

Pre-money valuation	$	9,000,000
Price per share	$	0.75
Shares offered		7,000,000
Money raised	$	**5,215,232**
Total shares outstanding		19,080,000
Post-money valuation	$	14,215,232

Ownership	Shares	%	Control
Founder 1	5,500,000	29%	
Founder 2	2,000,000	10%	52%
Founder 3	2,500,000	13%	
Early Angel	1,000,000	5%	
Angel	1,080,000	6%	
VC's	7,000,000	37%	
Total outstanding	19,080,000	100%	
Authorized shares remaining	920,000		

Shareholder	Shares	% Owned
Founder 1	5,500,000	28.89%
Founder 2	2,000,000	10.50%
Founder 3	2,500,000	13.13%
Early Angel 1	500,000	2.63%
Early Angel 2	500,000	2.63%
Angel 1	400,000	2.10%
Angel 2	400,000	2.10%
Angel 3	240,000	1.26%
VC 1	3,500,000	18.38%
VC 2	3,500,000	18.38%
	19,040,000	100.00%

This company stopped at this round of financing, but you can see how this could continue. In the next round the price would go up again, likely significantly, but it would still be a challenge for the founders to maintain 51% of the voting rights. Once the founders lose control of the company they must rely on being able to have 'friendly' investors vote with them on important issues. Suffice it to say, if the founders sell too much of the stock too soon then they may lose control early and risk being ejected from their own company. This is a very likely scenario for many entrepreneurs. They become tempted by the early, easy money and don't realize that they are sowing the seeds for future problems.

After many rounds of investment the cap table can become quite large. If the company finally goes public, then the cap table will list thousands of investors and millions of dollars. If you have directly purchased stock in any publicly traded company, then you are listed on a cap table somewhere in the finance department. Public companies, however, are also very heavily regulated and monitored so the process I am describing gets much, much more complex and nuanced.

APPENDIX E: SAMPLE TERM SHEET

This document was created by the National Venture Capital Association (NVCA) for educational purposes only. I am not giving legal advice. What follows is simply a very thorough example of a term sheet with explanatory footnotes. I highly encourage you to read each of the provisions and, before creating or signing any agreement, seek legal counsel.

(If you have trouble reading this document or would like a copy, please visit www.kchildreth.com/freedownloads)

This sample document is the work product of a national coalition of attorneys who specialize in venture capital financings, working under the auspices of the NVCA. This document is intended to serve as a starting point only, and should be tailored to meet your specific requirements. This document should not be construed as legal advice for any particular facts or circumstances. Note that this sample document presents an array of (often mutually exclusive) options with respect to particular deal provisions.

Preliminary Note

This term sheet maps to the NVCA Model Documents, and for convenience the provisions are grouped according to the particular Model Document in which they may be found. Although this term sheet is perhaps somewhat longer than a "typical" VC Term Sheet, the aim is to provide a level of detail that makes the term sheet useful as both a road map for the document drafters and as a reference source for the business people to quickly find deal terms without the necessity of having to consult the legal documents (assuming of course there have been no changes to the material deal terms prior to execution of the final documents).

TERM SHEET
FOR SERIES A PREFERRED STOCK FINANCING OF
[*INSERT COMPANY NAME*], INC.
[____ __, 20__]

This Term Sheet summarizes the principal terms of the Series A Preferred Stock Financing of [_____], Inc., a [Delaware] corporation (the "**Company**"). In consideration of the time and expense devoted and to be devoted by the Investors with respect to this investment, the No Shop/Confidentiality [and Counsel and Expenses] provisions of this Term Sheet shall be binding obligations of the Company whether or not the financing is consummated. No other legally binding obligations will be created until definitive agreements are executed and delivered by all parties. This Term Sheet is not a commitment to invest, and is conditioned on the completion of due diligence, legal review and documentation that is satisfactory to the Investors. This Term Sheet shall be governed in all respects by the laws of [_____the].[1]

Offering Terms

Closing Date:	As soon as practicable following the Company's acceptance of this Term Sheet and satisfaction of the Conditions to Closing (the

---

[1]   The choice of law governing a term sheet can be important because in some jurisdictions a term sheet that expressly states that it is nonbinding may nonetheless create an enforceable obligation to negotiate the terms set forth in the term sheet in good faith. Compare *SIGA Techs., Inc. v. PharmAthene, Inc., Case No. C.A. 2627 ((Del. Supreme Court May 24, 2013)* (holding that where parties agreed to negotiate in good faith in accordance with a term sheet, that obligation was enforceable notwithstanding the fact that the term sheet itself was not signed and contained a footer on each page stating "Non Binding Terms"); *EQT Infrastructure Ltd. v. Smith, 861 F. Supp. 2d 220 (S.D.N.Y. 2012); Stanford Hotels Corp. v. Potomac Creek Assocs., L.P., 18 A.3d 725 (D.C. App. 2011) with Rosenfield v. United States Trust Co.*, 5 N.E. 323, 326 (Mass. 1935) ("An agreement to reach an agreement is a contradiction in terms and imposes no obligation on the parties thereo."); *Martin v. Martin, 326 S.W.3d 741 (Tex. App. 2010); Va. Power Energy Mktg. v. EQT Energy, LLC, 2012 WL 2905110 (E.D. Va. July 16, 2012)*. As such, because a "nonbinding" term sheet governed by the law of a jurisdiction such as Delaware, New York or the District of Columbia may in fact create an enforceable obligation to negotiate in good faith to come to agreement on the terms set forth in the term sheet, parties should give consideration to the choice of law selected to govern the term sheet.

-1-

"**Closing**"). [*provide for multiple closings if applicable*]

Investors:

Investor No. 1: [_____] shares ([__]%), $[_____]

Investor No. 2: [_____] shares ([__]%), $[_____]

[as well other investors mutually agreed upon by Investors and the Company]

Amount Raised:

$[_____], [including $[_____] from the conversion of principal [and interest] on bridge notes].[2]

Price Per Share:

$[_____] per share (based on the capitalization of the Company set forth below) (the "**Original Purchase Price**").

Pre-Money Valuation:

The Original Purchase Price is based upon a fully-diluted pre-money valuation of $[____] and a fully-diluted post-money valuation of $[____] (including an employee pool representing [__]% of the fully-diluted post-money capitalization).

Capitalization:

The Company's capital structure before and after the Closing is set forth on Exhibit A.

CHARTER[3]

Dividends:

[*Alternative 1:* Dividends will be paid on the Series A Preferred on an as-converted basis when, as, and if paid on the Common Stock]

[*Alternative 2:* The Series A Preferred will carry an annual [__]% cumulative dividend [payable upon a liquidation or redemption]. For any other dividends or distributions, participation with Common Stock on an as-converted basis.][4]

[*Alternative 3:* Non-cumulative dividends will be paid on the Series A Preferred in an amount equal to $[____] per share of Series A Preferred when and if declared by the Board.]

---

[2]   Modify this provision to account for staged investments or investments dependent on the achievement of milestones by the Company.

[3]   The Charter (Certificate of Incorporation) is a public document, filed with the Secretary of State of the state in which the company is incorporated, that establishes all of the rights, preferences, privileges and restrictions of the Preferred Stock.

[4]   In some cases, accrued and unpaid dividends are payable on conversion as well as upon a liquidation event. Most typically, however, dividends are not paid if the preferred is converted. Another alternative is to give the Company the option to pay accrued and unpaid dividends in cash or in common shares valued at fair market value. The latter are referred to as "PIK" (payment-in-kind) dividends.

-2-

Liquidation Preference:	In the event of any liquidation, dissolution or winding up of the Company, the proceeds shall be paid as follows:

[*Alternative 1 (non-participating Preferred Stock)*: First pay [one] times the Original Purchase Price [plus accrued dividends] [plus declared and unpaid dividends] on each share of Series A Preferred (or, if greater, the amount that the Series A Preferred would receive on an as-converted basis). The balance of any proceeds shall be distributed pro rata to holders of Common Stock.]

[*Alternative 2 (full participating Preferred Stock)*: First pay [one] times the Original Purchase Price [plus accrued dividends] [plus declared and unpaid dividends] on each share of Series A Preferred. Thereafter, the Series A Preferred participates with the Common Stock pro rata on an as-converted basis.]

[*Alternative 3 (cap on Preferred Stock participation rights)*: First pay [one] times the Original Purchase Price [plus accrued dividends] [plus declared and unpaid dividends] on each share of Series A Preferred. Thereafter, Series A Preferred participates with Common Stock pro rata on an as-converted basis until the holders of Series A Preferred receive an aggregate of [_____] times the Original Purchase Price (including the amount paid pursuant to the preceding sentence).]

A merger or consolidation (other than one in which stockholders of the Company own a majority by voting power of the outstanding shares of the surviving or acquiring corporation) and a sale, lease, transfer, exclusive license or other disposition of all or substantially all of the assets of the Company will be treated as a liquidation event (a "**Deemed Liquidation Event**"), thereby triggering payment of the liquidation preferences described above [unless the holders of [___]% of the Series A Preferred elect otherwise]. [The Investors' entitlement to their liquidation preference shall not be abrogated or diminished in the event part of the consideration is subject to escrow in connection with a Deemed Liquidation Event.][5]

Voting Rights:	The Series A Preferred shall vote together with the Common Stock on an as-converted basis, and not as a separate class, except (i) [so long as [*insert fixed number, or %, or "any"*] shares of Series A Preferred are outstanding,] the Series A Preferred as a class shall be entitled to elect [_____] [(_)] members of the Board (the "**Series A Directors**"), and (ii) as required by law. The Company's

---

[5] See <u>Subsection 2.3.4</u> of the Model Certificate of Incorporation and the detailed explanation in related footnote 25.

-3-

Certificate of Incorporation will provide that the number of authorized shares of Common Stock may be increased or decreased with the approval of a majority of the Preferred and Common Stock, voting together as a single class, and without a separate class vote by the Common Stock.[6]

Protective Provisions:

[So long as [*insert fixed number, or %, or "any"*] shares of Series A Preferred are outstanding,] in addition to any other vote or approval required under the Company's Charter or Bylaws, the Company will not, without the written consent of the holders of at least [__]% of the Company's Series A Preferred, either directly or by amendment, merger, consolidation, or otherwise:

(i) liquidate, dissolve or wind-up the affairs of the Company, or effect any merger or consolidation or any other Deemed Liquidation Event; (ii) amend, alter, or repeal any provision of the Certificate of Incorporation or Bylaws [in a manner adverse to the Series A Preferred];[7] (iii) create or authorize the creation of or issue any other security convertible into or exercisable for any equity security, having rights, preferences or privileges senior to or on parity with the Series A Preferred, or increase the authorized number of shares of Series A Preferred; (iv) purchase or redeem or pay any dividend on any capital stock prior to the Series A Preferred, [other than stock repurchased from former employees or consultants in connection with the cessation of their employment/services, at the lower of fair market value or cost;] [other than as approved by the Board, including the approval of [____] Series A Director(s)]; or (v) create or authorize the creation of any debt security [if the Company's aggregate indebtedness would exceed $[___]][other than equipment leases or bank lines of credit][unless such debt security has received the prior approval of the Board of Directors, including the approval of [_____] Series A Director(s)]; (vi) create or hold capital stock in any subsidiary that is not a wholly-owned subsidiary or dispose of any subsidiary stock or all or substantially all of any subsidiary assets; [or (vii) increase or decrease the size of the Board of Directors].[8]

---

[6]   For corporations incorporated in California, one cannot "opt out" of the statutory requirement of a separate class vote by Common Stockholders to authorize shares of Common Stock. The purpose of this provision is to "opt out" of DGL 242(b)(2).

[7]   Note that as a matter of background law, Section 242(b)(2) of the Delaware General Corporation Law provides that if any proposed charter amendment would adversely alter the rights, preferences and powers of one series of Preferred Stock, but not similarly adversely alter the entire class of all Preferred Stock, then the holders of that series are entitled to a separate series vote on the amendment.

[8]   The board size provision may also be addressed in the Voting Agreement; see Section 1.1 of the Model Voting Agreement.

-4-

Optional Conversion:

The Series A Preferred initially converts 1:1 to Common Stock at any time at option of holder, subject to adjustments for stock dividends, splits, combinations and similar events and as described below under "Anti-dilution Provisions."

Anti-dilution Provisions:

In the event that the Company issues additional securities at a purchase price less than the current Series A Preferred conversion price, such conversion price shall be adjusted in accordance with the following formula:

[*Alternative 1:* "Typical" weighted average:

$$CP_2 = CP_1 * (A+B) / (A+C)$$

CP_2 = Series A Conversion Price in effect immediately after new issue

CP_1 = Series A Conversion Price in effect immediately prior to new issue

A = Number of shares of Common Stock deemed to be outstanding immediately prior to new issue (includes all shares of outstanding common stock, all shares of outstanding preferred stock on an as-converted basis, and all outstanding options on an as-exercised basis; and does not include any convertible securities converting into this round of financing)[9]

B = Aggregate consideration received by the Corporation with respect to the new issue divided by CP_1

C = Number of shares of stock issued in the subject transaction]

[*Alternative 2:* Full-ratchet – the conversion price will be reduced to the price at which the new shares are issued.]

[*Alternative 3:* No price-based anti-dilution protection.]

The following issuances shall not trigger anti-dilution adjustment:[10]

(i) securities issuable upon conversion of any of the Series A Preferred, or as a dividend or distribution on the Series A Preferred; (ii) securities issued upon the conversion of any debenture, warrant, option, or other convertible security; (iii) Common Stock issuable upon a stock split, stock dividend, or any subdivision of shares of Common Stock; and (iv) shares of

---

[9] The "broadest" base would include shares reserved in the option pool.

[10] Note that additional exclusions are frequently negotiated, such as issuances in connection with equipment leasing and commercial borrowing. See Subsections 4.4.1(d)(v)-(viii) of the Model Certificate of Incorporation for additional exclusions.

-5-

Common Stock (or options to purchase such shares of Common Stock) issued or issuable to employees or directors of, or consultants to, the Company pursuant to any plan approved by the Company's Board of Directors [including at least [_____] Series A Director(s)].

Mandatory Conversion:

Each share of Series A Preferred will automatically be converted into Common Stock at the then applicable conversion rate in the event of the closing of a [firm commitment] underwritten public offering with a price of [___] times the Original Purchase Price (subject to adjustments for stock dividends, splits, combinations and similar events) and [net/gross] proceeds to the Company of not less than $[_____] (a "**QPO**"), or (ii) upon the written consent of the holders of [__]% of the Series A Preferred.[11]

[Pay-to-Play:

[Unless the holders of [__]% of the Series A elect otherwise,] on any subsequent [down] round all [Major] Investors are required to purchase their pro rata share of the securities set aside by the Board for purchase by the [Major] Investors. All shares of Series A Preferred [12] of any [Major] Investor failing to do so will automatically [lose anti-dilution rights] [lose right to participate in future rounds] [convert to Common Stock and lose the right to a Board seat if applicable].][13]

Redemption Rights:[14]

Unless prohibited by Delaware law governing distributions to stockholders, the Series A Preferred shall be redeemable at the option of holders of at least [__]% of the Series A Preferred commencing any time after [_____] at a price equal to the Original Purchase Price [plus all accrued but unpaid dividends]. Redemption shall occur in three equal annual portions. Upon a redemption request from the holders of the required percentage of

---

[11]   The per share test ensures that the investor achieves a significant return on investment before the Company can go public. Also consider allowing a non-QPO to become a QPO if an adjustment is made to the Conversion Price for the benefit of the investor, so that the investor does not have the power to block a public offering.

[12]   Alternatively, this provision could apply on a proportionate basis (*e.g.*, if Investor plays for ½ of pro rata share, receives ½ of anti-dilution adjustment).

[13]   If the punishment for failure to participate is losing some but not all rights of the Preferred (*e.g.*, anything other than a forced conversion to common), the Certificate of Incorporation will need to have so-called "blank check preferred" provisions at least to the extent necessary to enable the Board to issue a "shadow" class of preferred with diminished rights in the event an investor fails to participate. Because these provisions flow through the charter, an alternative Model Certificate of Incorporation with "pay-to-play lite" provisions (*e.g.*, shadow Preferred) has been posted. As a drafting matter, it is far easier to simply have (some or all of) the preferred convert to common.

[14]   Redemption rights allow Investors to force the Company to redeem their shares at cost (and sometimes investors may also request a small guaranteed rate of return, in the form of a dividend). In practice, redemption rights are not often used; however, they do provide a form of exit and some possible leverage over the Company. While it is possible that the right to receive dividends on redemption could give rise to a Code Section 305 "deemed dividend" problem, many tax practitioners take the view that if the liquidation preference provisions in the Charter are drafted to provide that, on conversion, the holder receives the greater of its liquidation preference or its as-converted amount (as provided in the Model Certificate of Incorporation), then there is no Section 305 issue.

-6-

the Series A Preferred, all Series A Preferred shares shall be redeemed [(except for any Series A holders who affirmatively opt-out)].[15]

STOCK PURCHASE AGREEMENT

Representations and Warranties:

Standard representations and warranties by the Company. [Representations and warranties by Founders regarding technology ownership, etc.].[16]

Conditions to Closing:

Standard conditions to Closing, which shall include, among other things, satisfactory completion of financial and legal due diligence, qualification of the shares under applicable Blue Sky laws, the filing of a Certificate of Incorporation establishing the rights and preferences of the Series A Preferred, and an opinion of counsel to the Company.

Counsel and Expenses:

[Investor/Company] counsel to draft Closing documents. Company to pay all legal and administrative costs of the financing [at Closing], including reasonable fees (not to exceed $[____])and expenses of Investor counsel[, unless the transaction is not completed because the Investors withdraw their commitment without cause].[17]

Company Counsel: [_____
                      _____
                      _____]

Investor Counsel: [_____
                    _____
                    _____]

---

[15]   Due to statutory restrictions, the Company may not be legally permitted to redeem in the very circumstances where investors most want it (the so-called "sideways situation"). Accordingly, and particulary in light of the Delaware Chancery Court's ruling in *Thoughtworks* (see discussion in Model Charter), investors may seek enforcement provisions to give their redemption rights more teeth - *e.g.*, the holders of a majority of the Series A Preferred shall be entitled to elect a majority of the Company's Board of Directors, or shall have consent rights on Company cash expenditures, until such amounts are paid in full.

[16]   Founders' representations are controversial and may elicit significant resistance as they are found in a minority of venture deals. They are more likely to appear if Founders are receiving liquidity from the transaction, or if there is heightened concern over intellectual property (*e.g.*, the Company is a spin-out from an academic institution or the Founder was formerly with another company whose business could be deemed competitive with the Company), or in international deals. Founders' representations are even less common in subsequent rounds, where risk is viewed as significantly diminished and fairly shared by the investors, rather than being disproportionately borne by the Founders. A sample set of Founders Representations is attached as an Addendum at the end of the Model Stock Purchase Agreement.

[17]   The bracketed text should be deleted if this section is not designated in the introductory paragraph as one of the sections that is binding upon the Company regardless of whether the financing is consummated.

-7-

INVESTORS' RIGHTS AGREEMENT

Registration Rights:

Registrable Securities:	All shares of Common Stock issuable upon conversion of the Series A Preferred [and {any other Common Stock held by the Investors] will be deemed **"Registrable Securities**."[18]
Demand Registration:	Upon earliest of (i) [three-five] years after the Closing; or (ii) [six] months [19] following an initial public offering ("**IPO**"), persons holding [__]% of the Registrable Securities may request [one][two] (consummated) registrations by the Company of their shares. The aggregate offering price for such registration may not be less than $[5-15] million. A registration will count for this purpose only if (i) all Registrable Securities requested to be registered are registered, and (ii) it is closed, or withdrawn at the request of the Investors (other than as a result of a material adverse change to the Company).
Registration on Form S-3:	The holders of [10-30]% of the Registrable Securities will have the right to require the Company to register on Form S-3, if available for use by the Company, Registrable Securities for an aggregate offering price of at least $[1-5 million]. There will be no limit on the aggregate number of such Form S-3 registrations, provided that there are no more than [two] per year.
Piggyback Registration:	The holders of Registrable Securities will be entitled to "piggyback" registration rights on all registration statements of the Company, subject to the right, however, of the Company and its underwriters to reduce the number of shares proposed to be registered to a minimum of [20-30]% on a pro rata basis and to complete reduction on an IPO at the underwriter's discretion. In all events, the shares to be registered by holders of Registrable Securities will be reduced only after all other stockholders' shares are reduced.
Expenses:	The registration expenses (exclusive of stock transfer taxes, underwriting discounts and commissions will be borne by the Company. The Company will also pay the reasonable fees and expenses[, not to exceed $_____,] of one special counsel to represent all the participating stockholders.

---

[18] Note that Founders/management sometimes also seek limited registration rights.

[19] The Company will want the percentage to be high enough so that a significant portion of the investor base is behind the demand. Companies will typically resist allowing a single investor to cause a registration. Experienced investors will want to ensure that less experienced investors do not have the right to cause a demand registration. In some cases, different series of Preferred Stock may request the right for that series to initiate a certain number of demand registrations. Companies will typically resist this due to the cost and diversion of management resources when multiple constituencies have this right.

Lock-up:	Investors shall agree in connection with the IPO, if requested by the managing underwriter, not to sell or transfer any shares of Common Stock of the Company [(including/excluding shares acquired in or following the IPO)] for a period of up to 180 days [plus up to an additional 18 days to the extent necessary to comply with applicable regulatory requirements][20] following the IPO (provided all directors and officers of the Company [and [1 – 5]% stockholders] agree to the same lock-up). [Such lock-up agreement shall provide that any discretionary waiver or termination of the restrictions of such agreements by the Company or representatives of the underwriters shall apply to Investors, pro rata, based on the number of shares held.
Termination:	Upon a Deemed Liquidation Event, [and/or] when all shares of an Investor are eligible to be sold without restriction under Rule 144 [and/or] the [____] anniversary of the IPO.

No future registration rights may be granted without consent of the holders of a [majority] of the Registrable Securities unless subordinate to the Investor's rights. |
| *Management and Information Rights:* | A Management Rights letter from the Company, in a form reasonably acceptable to the Investors, will be delivered prior to Closing to each Investor that requests one.[21]

Any [Major] Investor [(who is not a competitor)] will be granted access to Company facilities and personnel during normal business hours and with reasonable advance notification. The Company will deliver to such Major Investor (i) annual, quarterly, [and monthly] financial statements, and other information as determined by the Board; (ii) thirty days prior to the end of each fiscal year, a comprehensive operating budget forecasting the Company's revenues, expenses, and cash position on a month-to-month basis for the upcoming fiscal year[; and (iii) promptly following the end of each quarter an up-to-date capitalization table. A "Major Investor" means any Investor who purchases at least $[_____] of Series A Preferred. |
| *Right to Participate Pro Rata in Future Rounds:* | All [Major] Investors shall have a pro rata right, based on their percentage equity ownership in the Company (assuming the conversion of all outstanding Preferred Stock into Common Stock and the exercise of all options outstanding under the Company's stock plans), to participate in subsequent issuances of equity securities of the Company (excluding those issuances listed at the |

---

[20] See commentary in footnotes 23 and 24 of the Model Investors' Rights Agreement regarding possible extensions of lock-up period.

[21] See commentary in introduction to Model Managements Rights Letter, explaining purpose of such letter.

*Matters Requiring Investor
Director Approval:*

end of the "Anti-dilution Provisions" section of this Term Sheet. In addition, should any [Major] Investor choose not to purchase its full pro rata share, the remaining [Major] Investors shall have the right to purchase the remaining pro rata shares.

[So long as the holders of Series A Preferred are entitled to elect a Series A Director, the Company will not, without Board approval, which approval must include the affirmative vote of [one/both] of the Series A Director(s):

(i) make any loan or advance to, or own any stock or other securities of, any subsidiary or other corporation, partnership, or other entity unless it is wholly owned by the Company; (ii) make any loan or advance to any person, including, any employee or director, except advances and similar expenditures in the ordinary course of business or under the terms of a employee stock or option plan approved by the Board of Directors; (iii) guarantee, any indebtedness except for trade accounts of the Company or any subsidiary arising in the ordinary course of business; (iv) make any investment inconsistent with any investment policy approved by the Board; (v) incur any aggregate indebtedness in excess of $[_____] that is not already included in a Board-approved budget, other than trade credit incurred in the ordinary course of business; (vi) enter into or be a party to any transaction with any director, officer or employee of the Company or any "associate" (as defined in Rule 12b-2 promulgated under the Exchange Act) of any such person [except transactions resulting in payments to or by the Company in an amount less than $[60,000] per year], [or transactions made in the ordinary course of business and pursuant to reasonable requirements of the Company's business and upon fair and reasonable terms that are approved by a majority of the Board of Directors];[22] (vii) hire, fire, or change the compensation of the executive officers, including approving any option grants; (viii) change the principal business of the Company, enter new lines of business, or exit the current line of business; (ix) sell, assign, license, pledge or encumber material technology or intellectual property, other than licenses granted in the ordinary course of business; or (x) enter into any corporate strategic relationship involving the payment contribution or assignment by the Company or to the Company of assets greater than [$100,000.00].

---

[22]   Note that Section 402 of the Sarbanes-Oxley Act of 2003 would require repayment of any loans in full prior to the Company filing a registration statement for an IPO.

Last Updated June 2013

Non-Competition and *Non-Solicitation Agreements:*[23]	Each Founder and key employee will enter into a [one] year non-competition and non-solicitation agreement in a form reasonably acceptable to the Investors.
Non-Disclosure and *Developments Agreement:*	Each current and former Founder, employee and consultant will enter into a non-disclosure and proprietary rights assignment agreement in a form reasonably acceptable to the Investors.
Board Matters:	[Each Board Committee shall include at least one Series A Director.]
	The Board of Directors shall meet at least [monthly][quarterly], unless otherwise agreed by a vote of the majority of Directors.
	The Company will bind D&O insurance with a carrier and in an amount satisfactory to the Board of Directors. Company to enter into Indemnification Agreement with each Series A Director [and affiliated funds] in form acceptable to such director. In the event the Company merges with another entity and is not the surviving corporation, or transfers all of its assets, proper provisions shall be made so that successors of the Company assume the Company's obligations with respect to indemnification of Directors.
Employee Stock Options:	All employee options to vest as follows: [25% after one year, with remaining vesting monthly over next 36 months].
	[Immediately prior to the Series A Preferred Stock investment, [_____] shares will be added to the option pool creating an unallocated option pool of [_____] shares.]
Key Person Insurance:	Company to acquire life insurance on Founders [*name each Founder*] in an amount satisfactory to the Board. Proceeds payable to the Company.

RIGHT OF FIRST REFUSAL/CO-SALE AGREEMENT

Right of First Refusal/ *Right of Co-Sale*	Company first and Investors second (to the extent assigned by the Board of Directors,) will have a right of first refusal with respect to any shares of capital stock of the Company proposed to be

---

[23] Note that non-compete restrictions (other than in connection with the sale of a business) are prohibited in California, and may not be enforceable in other jurisdictions, as well. In addition, some investors do not require such agreements for fear that employees will request additional consideration in exchange for signing a Non-Compete/Non-Solicit (and indeed the agreement may arguably be invalid absent such additional consideration - although having an employee sign a non-compete contemporaneous with hiring constitutes adequate consideration in jurisdictions where non-competes are generally enforceable). Others take the view that it should be up to the Board on a case-by-case basis to determine whether any particular key employee is required to sign such an agreement. Non-competes typically have a one year duration, although state law may permit up to two years. Note also that some states may require that a *new* Non-Compete be signed where there is a material change in the employee's duties/salary/title.

Last Updated June 2013

(Take-Me-Along):   transferred by Founders [and future employees holding greater than [1]% of Company Common Stock (assuming conversion of Preferred Stock and whether then held or subject to the exercise of options)], with a right of oversubscription for Investors of shares unsubscribed by the other Investors. Before any such person may sell Common Stock, he will give the Investors an opportunity to participate in such sale on a basis proportionate to the amount of securities held by the seller and those held by the participating Investors.[24]

VOTING AGREEMENT

Board of Directors: At the initial Closing, the Board shall consist of [_____] members comprised of (i) [*name*] as [the representative designated by [____], as the lead Investor, (ii) [*name*] as the representative designated by the remaining Investors, (iii) [*name*] as the representative designated by the Founders, (iv) the person then serving as the Chief Executive Officer of the Company, and (v) [___] person(s) who are not employed by the Company and who are mutually acceptable [to the Founders and Investors][to the other directors].

[Drag Along: Holders of Preferred Stock and the Founders [and all future holders of greater than [1]% of Common Stock (assuming conversion of Preferred Stock and whether then held or subject to the exercise of options)] shall be required to enter into an agreement with the Investors that provides that such stockholders will vote their shares in favor of a Deemed Liquidation Event or transaction in which 50% or more of the voting power of the Company is transferred and which is approved by [the Board of Directors] [and the holders of ____% of the outstanding shares of Preferred Stock, on an as-converted basis (the "**Electing Holders**")], so long as the liability of each stockholder in such transaction is several (and not joint) and does not exceed the stockholder's pro rata portion of any claim and the consideration to be paid to the stockholders in such transaction will be allocated as if the consideration were the proceeds to be distributed to the Company's stockholders in a liquidation under the Company's then-current Certificate of Incorporation.][25]

[Sale Rights: Upon written notice to the Company from the Electing Holders, the Company shall initiate a process intended to result in a sale of the Company.][26]

---

[24]   Certain exceptions are typically negotiated, *e.g.*, estate planning or *de minimis* transfers. Investors may also seek ROFR rights with respect to transfers by investors, in order to be able to have some control over the composition of the investor group.

[25]   See <u>Subsection 3.3</u> of the Model Voting Agreement for a more detailed list o f conditions that must be satisfied in order for the drag-along to be invoked.

[26]   See Addendum to Model Voting Agreement

-12-

OTHER MATTERS

Founders' Stock: All Founders to own stock outright subject to Company right to buyback at cost. Buyback right for [__]% for first [12 months] after Closing; thereafter, right lapses in equal [monthly] increments over following [__] months.

[Existing Preferred Stock:[27] The terms set forth above for the Series [_] Preferred Stock are subject to a review of the rights, preferences and restrictions for the existing Preferred Stock. Any changes necessary to conform the existing Preferred Stock to this term sheet will be made at the Closing.]

No Shop/Confidentiality: The Company agrees to work in good faith expeditiously towards a closing. The Company and the Founders agree that they will not, for a period of [_____] weeks from the date these terms are accepted, take any action to solicit, initiate, encourage or assist the submission of any proposal, negotiation or offer from any person or entity other than the Investors relating to the sale or issuance, of any of the capital stock of the Company [or the acquisition, sale, lease, license or other disposition of the Company or any material part of the stock or assets of the Company] and shall notify the Investors promptly of any inquiries by any third parties in regards to the foregoing. [In the event that the Company breaches this no-shop obligation and, prior to [_____], closes any of the above-referenced transactions [without providing the Investors the opportunity to invest on the same terms as the other parties to such transaction], then the Company shall pay to the Investors $[_____] upon the closing of any such transaction as liquidated damages.][28] The Company will not disclose the terms of this Term Sheet to any person other than officers, members of the Board of Directors and the Company's accountants and attorneys and other potential Investors acceptable to [_____], as lead Investor, without the written consent of the Investors.

Expiration: This Term Sheet expires on [_____ __, 20__] if not accepted by the Company by that date.

EXECUTED THIS [__] DAY OF [_____],20[___].

[SIGNATURE BLOCKS]

---

[27] Necessary only if this is a later round of financing, and not the initial Series A round.

[28] It is unusual to provide for such "break-up" fees in connection with a venture capital financing, but might be something to consider where there is a substantial possibility the Company may be sold prior to consummation of the financing (*e.g.*, a later stage deal).

-13-

Last Updated June 2013

EXHIBIT A

Pre and Post-Financing Capitalization

Security	Pre-Financing		Post-Financing	
	# of Shares	%	# of Shares	%
Common – Founders				
Common – Employee Stock Pool				
Issued				
Unissued				
[Common – Warrants]				
Series A Preferred				
Total				

APPENDIX F: USEFUL TERMS

Rather than repeat what has been done hundreds of times by many individuals and groups, I have listed below three websites (current as of the time of publication) that contain important terms you will hear as you encounter sophisticated investors. I encourage you to learn and use these terms. Like any profession, the investor and start-up world uses technical jargon that acts much like a secret password. Either you know the lingo or you don't…and this tells an investor or VC whether you 'get it' or not. If you don't 'get it', then you are deemed easy prey for hungry sharks!

http://www.altassets.net/private-equity-and-venture-capital-glossary-of-terms

http://www.fundingpost.com/glossary/venture-glossary.asp

http://www.mava.org/Entrepreneurs/Glossary-of-Terms.aspx

ABOUT THE AUTHOR

 K.C. HILDRETH is a successful entrepreneur, coach and business consultant who has founded or co-founded 8 companies, been a strategy and technology consultant to Fortune 50 telecommunications and financial services companies, and worked for the banking department of a major law firm on Wall Street and Capitol Hill. K.C. was one of the founders of a television technology company that sold for $80 million in 2005 and, in his various career incarnations, has occupied roles including board member, CEO, CTO, COO and investor…as well as salesperson, paralegal and stock-clerk.

K.C. holds a BA in Political Science from Ohio Wesleyan University, an MBA from The University of Virginia Darden School of Business, an MS in Information Systems from The University of Virginia McIntire School of Commerce, and an MA in Spiritual Psychology from the University of Santa Monica. K.C. writes, speaks and works with the deep belief that every person on this planet has a powerful gift, and can choose to use that gift to become greater than they ever imagined.

K.C. lives in Manhattan Beach, CA – www.kchildreth.com